Contents

Introduction	3
Veggie Deluxe	4
Green Machine	6
Plant Power Patty	8
Herbivore Burger	10
Vegan Classic	12
Lentil Lover	14
Mushroom Melt	16
Quinoa Quencher	18
Black Bean Beauty	20
Chickpea Sensation	22
Sweet Potato Surprise	24
Tempeh Tango	26
Seitan Supreme	28
Tofu Twist	30
Walnut Wonder	32
Zesty Zucchini	34
Spicy Sriracha	36
Mediterranean Marvel	38
Thai Fusion	40
Mexican Fiesta	42
Curry Creation	44
Falafel Fantasy	46
Jackfruit Joy	48
Portobello Perfection	50
Hawaiian Luau	52
Pesto Passion	54

Greek Goddess	**56**
Smoky Chipotle	**58**
Teriyaki Temptation	**60**
Spinach Surprise	**62**
CILANTRO LIME	**64**
Avocado Delight	**66**
Sundried Tomato Special	**68**
Basil Bomb	**70**
Ginger Glaze	**72**
Peanut Butter Patty	**74**
Moroccan Magic	**76**
Cajun Craze	**78**
Truffle Tremor	**80**
Caramelized Onion	**82**
Balsamic Bliss	**84**
Salsa Sensation	**86**
Asian Fusion	**88**
Herb Garden	**90**
Chipotle Kick	**92**
Sweet Chili Surprise	**94**
Smoky Maple	**96**

Introduction

Welcome to the world of vegan burgers, where plant-based ingredients are transformed into mouthwatering, flavor-packed creations that will redefine your perception of what a burger can be. Welcome on a culinary journey that celebrates the vibrant and diverse world of plant-based eating, with a focus on one of the most beloved comfort foods—the burger.

The mission is simple: to prove that plant-based burgers can be just as satisfying, flavorful, and satisfyingly hearty as their meat counterparts. Vegan cooking is not about deprivation or sacrifice but rather an opportunity to explore a world of possibilities. The aim of this book is to show you the incredible versatility of plant-based ingredients and how they can be combined to create innovative, delicious, and nutritionally balanced burgers that will leave you craving for more.

But this cookbook is not just about recipes—it's also about embracing a lifestyle that is compassionate, sustainable, and nourishing. We'll share tips and tricks for sourcing the freshest ingredients, selecting the right cooking techniques, and even making your own homemade condiments and spreads. Moreover, we'll delve into the nutritional benefits of plant-based eating, showcasing how these burgers can contribute to your overall health and well-being.

So, grab your apron, fire up the stove, and let's dive into the world of vegan burgers. Get ready to savor the delectable flavors, indulge in the satisfying textures, and discover a whole new realm of plant-based deliciousness. Let this cookbook be your guide as you embark on a culinary adventure that will delight your senses, nourish your body, and ignite your passion for vegan cooking.

Veggie Deluxe

INGREDIENTS:

1 cup cooked quinoa
1 cup cooked black beans, mashed
1 small onion, finely chopped
2 cloves garlic, minced
1 medium carrot, grated
1/2 red bell pepper, finely chopped
1/4 cup chopped fresh parsley
1/4 cup bread crumbs (use gluten-free if necessary)
2 tablespoons ground flaxseed mixed with 3 tablespoons water (flax egg)
1 tablespoon soy sauce or tamari
1 teaspoon smoked paprika
1/2 teaspoon ground cumin
Salt and pepper to taste
Burger buns
Toppings of your choice (lettuce, tomato, onion, avocado, vegan cheese, etc.)
Condiments of your choice (vegan mayo, ketchup, mustard, etc.)

INSTRUCTIONS:

In a large mixing bowl, combine the mashed black beans, cooked quinoa, chopped onion, minced garlic, grated carrot, chopped red bell pepper, parsley, bread crumbs, flax egg, soy sauce, smoked paprika, cumin, salt, and pepper. Mix well until all ingredients are evenly combined.

Allow the mixture to sit for about 10 minutes to let the flavors meld together and the breadcrumbs and flax egg to bind the mixture.

Divide the mixture into equal portions and shape each portion into a patty of your desired size and thickness.

Heat a non-stick skillet or grill pan over medium heat. Lightly grease the pan with oil or cooking spray.

Place the burger patties onto the preheated pan and cook for about 4-5 minutes on each side, or until they develop a golden brown crust. You can also grill the patties on an outdoor grill if preferred.

While the patties are cooking, you can toast the burger buns if desired.

Once the patties are cooked, remove them from the heat and let them cool slightly.

Assemble your burgers by placing each patty on a toasted bun. Add your favorite toppings such as lettuce, tomato, onion, avocado, vegan cheese, and condiments like vegan mayo, ketchup, or mustard.

Serve "The Veggie Deluxe" vegan burgers with a side of sweet potato fries, a salad, or any other accompaniments of your choice.

Green Machine

INGREDIENTS:

1 cup cooked quinoa
1 cup cooked green lentils, mashed
1 small onion, finely chopped
2 cloves garlic, minced
1 cup packed spinach, finely chopped
1/4 cup chopped fresh cilantro
1/4 cup bread crumbs (use gluten-free if necessary)
2 tablespoons ground flaxseed mixed with 3 tablespoons water (flax egg)
1 tablespoon soy sauce or tamari
1 teaspoon ground cumin
1/2 teaspoon turmeric
Salt and pepper to taste
Burger buns
Toppings of your choice (lettuce, sprouts, cucumber, avocado, vegan mayo, etc.)
Condiments of your choice (salsa, tahini sauce, vegan yogurt, etc.)

INSTRUCTIONS:

In a large mixing bowl, combine the mashed green lentils, cooked quinoa, chopped onion, minced garlic, chopped spinach, cilantro, bread crumbs, flax egg, soy sauce, cumin, turmeric, salt, and pepper. Mix well until all ingredients are evenly combined.

Allow the mixture to sit for about 10 minutes to let the flavors meld together and the breadcrumbs and flax egg to bind the mixture.

Divide the mixture into equal portions and shape each portion into a patty of your desired size and thickness.

Heat a non-stick skillet or grill pan over medium heat. Lightly grease the pan with oil or cooking spray.

Place the burger patties onto the preheated pan and cook for about 4-5 minutes on each side, or until they develop a golden brown crust. You can also grill the patties on an outdoor grill if preferred.

While the patties are cooking, you can toast the burger buns if desired.

Once the patties are cooked, remove them from the heat and let them cool slightly.

Assemble your burgers by placing each patty on a toasted bun. Add your favorite toppings such as lettuce, sprouts, cucumber slices, avocado, and condiments like vegan mayo, salsa, tahini sauce, or vegan yogurt.

Serve "The Green Machine" vegan burgers with a side of oven-baked sweet potato fries or a fresh salad for a complete meal.

Plant Power Patty

INGREDIENTS:

1 cup cooked quinoa
1 cup cooked chickpeas, mashed
1 small onion, finely chopped
2 cloves garlic, minced
1 medium carrot, grated
1/2 cup rolled oats
1/4 cup chopped fresh parsley
2 tablespoons nutritional yeast
2 tablespoons tomato paste
1 tablespoon soy sauce or tamari
1 teaspoon ground cumin
1/2 teaspoon smoked paprika
Salt and pepper to taste
Burger buns
Toppings of your choice (sliced tomato, lettuce, onion, pickles, vegan cheese, etc.)
Condiments of your choice (vegan mayo, ketchup, mustard, etc.)

INSTRUCTIONS:

In a large mixing bowl, combine the mashed chickpeas, cooked quinoa, chopped onion, minced garlic, grated carrot, rolled oats, parsley, nutritional yeast, tomato paste, soy sauce, cumin, smoked paprika, salt, and pepper. Mix well until all ingredients are evenly combined.

Allow the mixture to sit for about 10 minutes to let the flavors meld together and the oats to absorb some moisture.

Divide the mixture into equal portions and shape each portion into a patty of your desired size and thickness.

Heat a non-stick skillet or grill pan over medium heat. Lightly grease the pan with oil or cooking spray.

Place the burger patties onto the preheated pan and cook for about 4-5 minutes on each side, or until they develop a golden brown crust. You can also grill the patties on an outdoor grill if preferred.

While the patties are cooking, you can toast the burger buns if desired.

Once the patties are cooked, remove them from the heat and let them cool slightly.

Assemble your burgers by placing each patty on a toasted bun. Add your favorite toppings such as sliced tomato, lettuce, onion, pickles, and condiments like vegan mayo, ketchup, or mustard.

Serve "The Plant Power Patty" vegan burgers with a side of oven-baked sweet potato wedges or a crisp salad for a satisfying meal.

Herbivore Burger

INGREDIENTS:

1 cup cooked quinoa
1 cup cooked black beans, mashed
1 small onion, finely chopped
2 cloves garlic, minced
1/2 cup chopped mushrooms (such as cremini or button mushrooms)
1/4 cup chopped fresh parsley
2 tablespoons nutritional yeast
2 tablespoons ground flaxseed mixed with 3 tablespoons water (flax egg)
1 tablespoon soy sauce or tamari
1 teaspoon dried thyme
1/2 teaspoon dried rosemary
Salt and pepper to taste
Burger buns
Toppings of your choice (sliced tomato, lettuce, onion, avocado, vegan cheese, etc.)
Condiments of your choice (vegan mayo, ketchup, mustard, etc.)

INSTRUCTIONS:

In a large mixing bowl, combine the mashed black beans, cooked quinoa, chopped onion, minced garlic, chopped mushrooms, parsley, nutritional yeast, flax egg, soy sauce, dried thyme, dried rosemary, salt, and pepper. Mix well until all ingredients are evenly combined.

Allow the mixture to sit for about 10 minutes to let the flavors meld together and the flax egg to bind the mixture.

Divide the mixture into equal portions and shape each portion into a patty of your desired size and thickness.

Heat a non-stick skillet or grill pan over medium heat. Lightly grease the pan with oil or cooking spray.

Place the burger patties onto the preheated pan and cook for about 4-5 minutes on each side, or until they develop a golden brown crust. You can also grill the patties on an outdoor grill if preferred.

While the patties are cooking, you can toast the burger buns if desired.

Once the patties are cooked, remove them from the heat and let them cool slightly.

Assemble your burgers by placing each patty on a toasted bun. Add your favorite toppings such as sliced tomato, lettuce, onion, avocado, and condiments like vegan mayo, ketchup, or mustard.

Serve "The Herbivore Burger" vegan burgers with a side of baked sweet potato fries or a fresh salad for a complete meal.

Vegan Classic

INGREDIENTS:

1 cup cooked lentils (green or brown), drained
1 cup cooked quinoa
1 small onion, finely chopped
2 cloves garlic, minced
1/4 cup bread crumbs (use gluten-free if necessary)
2 tablespoons ground flaxseed mixed with 3 tablespoons water (flax egg)
2 tablespoons tomato paste
1 tablespoon soy sauce or tamari
1 teaspoon smoked paprika
1/2 teaspoon ground cumin
Salt and pepper to taste
Burger buns
Toppings of your choice (lettuce, tomato, onion, pickles, vegan cheese, etc.)
Condiments of your choice (vegan mayo, ketchup, mustard, etc.)

INSTRUCTIONS:

In a large mixing bowl, combine the cooked lentils, cooked quinoa, chopped onion, minced garlic, bread crumbs, flax egg, tomato paste, soy sauce, smoked paprika, cumin, salt, and pepper. Mix well until all ingredients are evenly combined.

Allow the mixture to sit for about 10 minutes to let the flavors meld together and the bread crumbs and flax egg to bind the mixture.

Divide the mixture into equal portions and shape each portion into a patty of your desired size and thickness.

Heat a non-stick skillet or grill pan over medium heat. Lightly grease the pan with oil or cooking spray.

Place the burger patties onto the preheated pan and cook for about 4-5 minutes on each side, or until they develop a golden brown crust. You can also grill the patties on an outdoor grill if preferred.

While the patties are cooking, you can toast the burger buns if desired.

Once the patties are cooked, remove them from the heat and let them cool slightly.

Assemble your burgers by placing each patty on a toasted bun. Add your favorite toppings such as lettuce, tomato, onion, pickles, and condiments like vegan mayo, ketchup, or mustard.

Serve "The Vegan Classic" burgers with a side of oven-baked potato wedges or a fresh salad for a complete meal.

Lentil Lover

INGREDIENTS:

1 cup cooked green or brown lentils
1 small onion, finely chopped
2 cloves garlic, minced
1 carrot, grated
1/2 cup rolled oats
1/4 cup chopped fresh parsley
2 tablespoons tomato paste
2 tablespoons nutritional yeast
1 tablespoon soy sauce or tamari
1 teaspoon ground cumin
1/2 teaspoon smoked paprika
Salt and pepper to taste
Burger buns
Toppings of your choice (lettuce, tomato, onion, pickles, vegan cheese, etc.)
Condiments of your choice (vegan mayo, ketchup, mustard, etc.)

INSTRUCTIONS:

In a large mixing bowl, combine the cooked lentils, chopped onion, minced garlic, grated carrot, rolled oats, parsley, tomato paste, nutritional yeast, soy sauce, cumin, smoked paprika, salt, and pepper. Mix well until all ingredients are evenly combined.

Allow the mixture to sit for about 10 minutes to let the flavors meld together and the oats to absorb some moisture.

Divide the mixture into equal portions and shape each portion into a patty of your desired size and thickness.

Heat a non-stick skillet or grill pan over medium heat. Lightly grease the pan with oil or cooking spray.

Place the burger patties onto the preheated pan and cook for about 4-5 minutes on each side, or until they develop a golden brown crust. You can also grill the patties on an outdoor grill if preferred.

While the patties are cooking, you can toast the burger buns if desired.

Once the patties are cooked, remove them from the heat and let them cool slightly.

Assemble your burgers by placing each patty on a toasted bun. Add your favorite toppings such as lettuce, tomato, onion, pickles, and condiments like vegan mayo, ketchup, or mustard.

Serve "The Lentil Lover" vegan burgers with a side of oven-baked potato wedges, a fresh salad, or any other side dish of your choice.

Mushroom Melt

INGREDIENTS:

2 portobello mushroom caps
2 tablespoons balsamic vinegar
2 tablespoons soy sauce or tamari
2 tablespoons olive oil
2 garlic cloves, minced
Salt and pepper to taste
Burger buns
Vegan cheese slices (such as vegan cheddar or mozzarella)
Toppings of your choice (lettuce, tomato, onion, pickles, etc.)
Condiments of your choice (vegan mayo, ketchup, mustard, etc.)

INSTRUCTIONS:

In a small bowl, whisk together the balsamic vinegar, soy sauce, olive oil, minced garlic, salt, and pepper.

Place the portobello mushroom caps in a shallow dish or zip-top bag. Pour the marinade over the mushrooms and ensure they are well coated. Allow them to marinate for at least 30 minutes, flipping them halfway through to ensure even marination.

Preheat a grill or grill pan to medium-high heat.

Remove the mushrooms from the marinade, reserving the marinade for later use.

Place the mushrooms on the preheated grill or grill pan and cook for about 4-5 minutes on each side, or until they are tender and cooked through. Baste the mushrooms with the reserved marinade during cooking.

While the mushrooms are cooking, you can toast the burger buns if desired.

Once the mushrooms are cooked, remove them from the heat and place a slice of vegan cheese on each mushroom cap. Allow the cheese to melt slightly from the residual heat.

Assemble your burgers by placing each mushroom cap on a toasted bun. Add your favorite toppings such as lettuce, tomato, onion, pickles, and condiments like vegan mayo, ketchup, or mustard.

Serve "The Mushroom Melt" vegan burgers with a side of oven-baked fries, a salad, or any other accompaniments you prefer.

Quinoa Quencher

INGREDIENTS:

1 cup cooked quinoa
1 can black beans, drained and rinsed
1 small onion, finely chopped
2 cloves garlic, minced
1/2 cup corn kernels (fresh or frozen)
1/4 cup chopped fresh cilantro
2 tablespoons ground flaxseed mixed with 3 tablespoons water (flax egg)
2 tablespoons nutritional yeast
1 tablespoon soy sauce or tamari
1 teaspoon ground cumin
1/2 teaspoon chili powder
Salt and pepper to taste
Burger buns
Toppings of your choice (lettuce, tomato, onion, avocado, etc.)
Condiments of your choice (vegan mayo, ketchup, mustard, etc.)

INSTRUCTIONS:

In a large mixing bowl, combine the cooked quinoa, black beans, chopped onion, minced garlic, corn kernels, cilantro, flax egg, nutritional yeast, soy sauce, cumin, chili powder, salt, and pepper. Mix well until all ingredients are evenly combined.

Allow the mixture to sit for about 10 minutes to let the flavors meld together and the flax egg to bind the mixture.

Divide the mixture into equal portions and shape each portion into a patty of your desired size and thickness.

Heat a non-stick skillet or grill pan over medium heat. Lightly grease the pan with oil or cooking spray.

Place the burger patties onto the preheated pan and cook for about 4-5 minutes on each side, or until they develop a golden brown crust. You can also grill the patties on an outdoor grill if preferred.

While the patties are cooking, you can toast the burger buns if desired.

Once the patties are cooked, remove them from the heat and let them cool slightly.

Assemble your burgers by placing each patty on a toasted bun. Add your favorite toppings such as lettuce, tomato, onion, avocado, and condiments like vegan mayo, ketchup, or mustard.

Serve "The Quinoa Quencher" vegan burgers with a side of sweet potato fries, a salad, or any other side dish you prefer.

Black Bean Beauty

INGREDIENTS:

1 can black beans, drained and rinsed
1 small onion, finely chopped
2 cloves garlic, minced
1/2 cup rolled oats
1/4 cup chopped fresh cilantro
2 tablespoons tomato paste
1 tablespoon ground flaxseed mixed with 3 tablespoons water (flax egg)
1 teaspoon ground cumin
1/2 teaspoon chili powder
Salt and pepper to taste
Burger buns
Toppings of your choice (lettuce, tomato, onion, avocado, etc.)
Condiments of your choice (vegan mayo, ketchup, mustard, etc.)

INSTRUCTIONS:

In a large mixing bowl, mash the black beans with a fork or potato masher until they are mostly mashed but still have some texture.

Add the chopped onion, minced garlic, rolled oats, cilantro, tomato paste, flax egg, cumin, chili powder, salt, and pepper to the bowl. Mix well until all ingredients are thoroughly combined.

Allow the mixture to sit for about 10 minutes to let the flavors meld together and the oats to absorb some moisture.

Divide the mixture into equal portions and shape each portion into a patty of your desired size and thickness.

Heat a non-stick skillet or grill pan over medium heat. Lightly grease the pan with oil or cooking spray.

Place the burger patties onto the preheated pan and cook for about 4-5 minutes on each side, or until they develop a golden brown crust. You can also grill the patties on an outdoor grill if preferred.

While the patties are cooking, you can toast the burger buns if desired.

Once the patties are cooked, remove them from the heat and let them cool slightly.

Assemble your burgers by placing each patty on a toasted bun. Add your favorite toppings such as lettuce, tomato, onion, avocado, and condiments like vegan mayo, ketchup, or mustard.

Serve "The Black Bean Beauty" vegan burgers with a side of oven-baked sweet potato fries, a fresh salad, or any other accompaniments you prefer.

Chickpea Sensation

INGREDIENTS:

1 can chickpeas, drained and rinsed
1 small onion, finely chopped
2 cloves garlic, minced
1/4 cup chopped fresh parsley
2 tablespoons tahini
2 tablespoons chickpea flour (or any other flour of your choice)
1 tablespoon lemon juice
1 teaspoon ground cumin
1/2 teaspoon paprika
Salt and pepper to taste
Burger buns
Toppings of your choice (lettuce, tomato, onion, avocado, etc.)
Condiments of your choice (vegan mayo, ketchup, mustard, etc.)

INSTRUCTIONS:

In a food processor, pulse the chickpeas until they are roughly mashed but still have some texture. Alternatively, you can mash them with a fork or potato masher.

In a large mixing bowl, combine the mashed chickpeas, chopped onion, minced garlic, parsley, tahini, chickpea flour, lemon juice, cumin, paprika, salt, and pepper. Mix well until all ingredients are evenly combined.

Allow the mixture to sit for about 10 minutes to let the flavors meld together and the chickpea flour to bind the mixture.

Divide the mixture into equal portions and shape each portion into a patty of your desired size and thickness.

Heat a non-stick skillet or grill pan over medium heat. Lightly grease the pan with oil or cooking spray.

Place the burger patties onto the preheated pan and cook for about 4-5 minutes on each side, or until they develop a golden brown crust. You can also grill the patties on an outdoor grill if preferred.

While the patties are cooking, you can toast the burger buns if desired.

Once the patties are cooked, remove them from the heat and let them cool slightly.

Assemble your burgers by placing each patty on a toasted bun. Add your favorite toppings such as lettuce, tomato, onion, avocado, and condiments like vegan mayo, ketchup, or mustard.

Serve "The Chickpea Sensation" vegan burgers with a side of oven-baked potato wedges, a fresh salad, or any other accompaniments you prefer.

Sweet Potato Surprise

INGREDIENTS:

1 large sweet potato, peeled and grated
1 can black beans, drained and rinsed
1 small onion, finely chopped
2 cloves garlic, minced
1/4 cup rolled oats
2 tablespoons ground flaxseed mixed with 3 tablespoons water (flax egg)
2 tablespoons nutritional yeast
1 teaspoon ground cumin
1/2 teaspoon smoked paprika
Salt and pepper to taste
Burger buns
Toppings of your choice (lettuce, tomato, onion, avocado, etc.)
Condiments of your choice (vegan mayo, ketchup, mustard, etc.)

INSTRUCTIONS:

Preheat the oven to 400°F (200°C).

In a large mixing bowl, combine the grated sweet potato, mashed black beans (you can mash them with a fork or pulse them briefly in a food processor), chopped onion, minced garlic, rolled oats, flax egg, nutritional yeast, cumin, smoked paprika, salt, and pepper. Mix well until all ingredients are thoroughly combined.

Allow the mixture to sit for about 10 minutes to let the oats absorb some moisture and bind the mixture.

Shape the mixture into equal-sized patties of your desired size and thickness.

Place the patties on a baking sheet lined with parchment paper and bake in the preheated oven for about 20-25 minutes, flipping them halfway through, or until they are golden brown and crispy on the outside.

While the patties are baking, you can toast the burger buns if desired.

Once the patties are cooked, remove them from the oven and let them cool slightly.

Assemble your burgers by placing each patty on a toasted bun. Add your favorite toppings such as lettuce, tomato, onion, avocado, and condiments like vegan mayo, ketchup, or mustard.

Serve "The Sweet Potato Surprise" vegan burgers with a side of baked sweet potato fries, a fresh salad, or any other accompaniments you prefer.

Tempeh Tango

INGREDIENTS:

8 ounces (225g) tempeh, crumbled
1 small onion, finely chopped
2 cloves garlic, minced
1 tablespoon soy sauce or tamari
1 tablespoon tomato paste
1 tablespoon nutritional yeast
1 teaspoon ground cumin
1/2 teaspoon smoked paprika
1/4 teaspoon chili powder (optional for extra heat)
Salt and pepper to taste
2 tablespoons olive oil
Burger buns
Toppings of your choice (lettuce, tomato, onion, avocado, etc.)
Condiments of your choice (vegan mayo, ketchup, mustard, etc.)

INSTRUCTIONS:

In a food processor, pulse the crumbled tempeh until it reaches a crumbly, ground meat-like texture. Alternatively, you can crumble it by hand.

In a large mixing bowl, combine the tempeh, chopped onion, minced garlic, soy sauce, tomato paste, nutritional yeast, cumin, smoked paprika, chili powder (if using), salt, and pepper. Mix well until all ingredients are evenly combined.

Allow the mixture to sit for about 10 minutes to let the flavors meld together.

Shape the mixture into equal-sized patties of your desired size and thickness.

Heat the olive oil in a skillet over medium heat.

Place the patties onto the preheated skillet and cook for about 4-5 minutes on each side, or until they develop a golden brown crust.

While the patties are cooking, you can toast the burger buns if desired.

Once the patties are cooked, remove them from the heat and let them cool slightly.

Assemble your burgers by placing each patty on a toasted bun. Add your favorite toppings such as lettuce, tomato, onion, avocado, and condiments like vegan mayo, ketchup, or mustard.

Serve "The Tempeh Tango" vegan burgers with a side of oven-baked potato wedges, a fresh salad, or any other accompaniments you prefer.

Seitan Supreme

INGREDIENTS:

1 cup vital wheat gluten
1/4 cup nutritional yeast
2 tablespoons chickpea flour (or any other flour of your choice)
1 teaspoon onion powder
1 teaspoon garlic powder
1/2 teaspoon smoked paprika
1/2 teaspoon dried thyme
1/2 teaspoon dried oregano
1/2 teaspoon salt
1/4 teaspoon black pepper
3/4 cup vegetable broth
2 tablespoons soy sauce or tamari
1 tablespoon tomato paste
2 cloves garlic, minced
1 tablespoon olive oil
Burger buns
Toppings of your choice (lettuce, tomato, onion, avocado, etc.)
Condiments of your choice (vegan mayo, ketchup, mustard, etc.)

INSTRUCTIONS:

In a large mixing bowl, combine the vital wheat gluten, nutritional yeast, chickpea flour, onion powder, garlic powder, smoked paprika, dried thyme, dried oregano, salt, and black pepper. Mix well to ensure the dry ingredients are evenly combined.

In a separate bowl, whisk together the vegetable broth, soy sauce or tamari, tomato paste, minced garlic, and olive oil.

Pour the wet ingredients into the bowl with the dry ingredients. Stir until the mixture forms a dough.

Knead the dough for about 3-4 minutes to develop the gluten and create a firm texture.

Divide the dough into equal-sized portions and shape each portion into a patty of your desired size and thickness.

Heat a non-stick skillet or grill pan over medium heat. Lightly grease the pan with oil or cooking spray.

Place the seitan patties onto the preheated pan and cook for about 6-8 minutes on each side, or until they are firm and golden brown.

While the patties are cooking, you can toast the burger buns if desired.

Once the patties are cooked, remove them from the heat and let them cool slightly.

Assemble your burgers by placing each patty on a toasted bun. Add your favorite toppings such as lettuce, tomato, onion, avocado, and condiments like vegan mayo, ketchup, or mustard.

Serve "The Seitan Supreme" vegan burgers with a side of crispy oven-baked potato wedges, a fresh salad, or any other accompaniments you prefer.

Tofu Twist

INGREDIENTS:

14 ounces (400g) firm tofu, drained and pressed
1/4 cup breadcrumbs (use gluten-free breadcrumbs if needed)
2 tablespoons nutritional yeast
2 tablespoons soy sauce or tamari
1 tablespoon tomato paste
1 teaspoon garlic powder
1/2 teaspoon smoked paprika
1/2 teaspoon ground cumin
1/4 teaspoon turmeric powder
Salt and pepper to taste
Burger buns
Toppings of your choice (lettuce, tomato, onion, avocado, etc.)
Condiments of your choice (vegan mayo, ketchup, mustard, etc.)

INSTRUCTIONS:

Preheat the oven to 375°F (190°C).

In a large mixing bowl, crumble the pressed tofu using your hands or a fork until it resembles a ground meat-like texture.

Add the breadcrumbs, nutritional yeast, soy sauce or tamari, tomato paste, garlic powder, smoked paprika, ground cumin, turmeric powder, salt, and pepper to the bowl. Mix well until all ingredients are evenly combined.

Allow the mixture to sit for about 10 minutes to let the flavors meld together.

Shape the mixture into equal-sized patties of your desired size and thickness.

Place the patties on a baking sheet lined with parchment paper and bake in the preheated oven for about 25-30 minutes, flipping them halfway through, or until they are firm and golden brown.

While the patties are baking, you can toast the burger buns if desired.

Once the patties are cooked, remove them from the oven and let them cool slightly.

Assemble your burgers by placing each patty on a toasted bun. Add your favorite toppings such as lettuce, tomato, onion, avocado, and condiments like vegan mayo, ketchup, or mustard.

Serve "The Tofu Twist" vegan burgers with a side of oven-baked sweet potato fries, a fresh salad, or any other accompaniments you prefer.

Walnut Wonder

INGREDIENTS:

1 cup walnuts
1 cup cooked quinoa
1 small onion, finely chopped
2 cloves garlic, minced
2 tablespoons ground flaxseed mixed with 3 tablespoons water (flax egg)
2 tablespoons nutritional yeast
1 tablespoon soy sauce or tamari
1 teaspoon ground cumin
1/2 teaspoon smoked paprika
1/4 teaspoon chili powder (optional for extra heat)
Salt and pepper to taste
Burger buns
Toppings of your choice (lettuce, tomato, onion, avocado, etc.)
Condiments of your choice (vegan mayo, ketchup, mustard, etc.)

INSTRUCTIONS:

Preheat the oven to 350°F (175°C).

In a food processor, pulse the walnuts until they reach a coarse texture. Be careful not to over-process and turn them into a paste.

In a large mixing bowl, combine the pulsed walnuts, cooked quinoa, chopped onion, minced garlic, flax egg, nutritional yeast, soy sauce or tamari, cumin, smoked paprika, chili powder (if using), salt, and pepper. Mix well until all ingredients are thoroughly combined.

Allow the mixture to sit for about 10 minutes to let the flavors meld together and the mixture to bind slightly.

Shape the mixture into equal-sized patties of your desired size and thickness.

Heat a non-stick skillet or grill pan over medium heat. Lightly grease the pan with oil or cooking spray.

Place the walnut patties onto the preheated pan and cook for about 4-5 minutes on each side, or until they develop a golden brown crust.

While the patties are cooking, you can toast the burger buns if desired.

Once the patties are cooked, remove them from the heat and let them cool slightly.

Assemble your burgers by placing each patty on a toasted bun. Add your favorite toppings such as lettuce, tomato, onion, avocado, and condiments like vegan mayo, ketchup, or mustard.

Serve "The Walnut Wonder" vegan burgers with a side of oven-baked sweet potato wedges, a fresh salad, or any other accompaniments you prefer.

Zesty Zucchini

INGREDIENTS:

2 medium zucchini, grated and squeezed to remove excess moisture
1 cup cooked quinoa
1/2 cup rolled oats
1/4 cup sunflower seeds
1/4 cup finely chopped fresh herbs (such as parsley, basil, or cilantro)
2 tablespoons nutritional yeast
1 tablespoon lemon zest
1 teaspoon ground cumin
1/2 teaspoon garlic powder
Salt and pepper to taste
Burger buns
Toppings of your choice (lettuce, tomato, onion, avocado, etc.)
Condiments of your choice (vegan mayo, ketchup, mustard, etc.)

INSTRUCTIONS:

Preheat the oven to 375°F (190°C).

Place the grated zucchini in a clean kitchen towel and squeeze out the excess moisture over the sink.

In a large mixing bowl, combine the squeezed zucchini, cooked quinoa, rolled oats, sunflower seeds, chopped fresh herbs, nutritional yeast, lemon zest, cumin, garlic powder, salt, and pepper. Mix well until all ingredients are evenly combined.

Allow the mixture to sit for about 10 minutes to let the oats absorb some moisture and bind the mixture.

Shape the mixture into equal-sized patties of your desired size and thickness.

Place the patties on a baking sheet lined with parchment paper and bake in the preheated oven for about 25-30 minutes, flipping them halfway through, or until they are golden brown and firm.

While the patties are baking, you can toast the burger buns if desired.

Once the patties are cooked, remove them from the oven and let them cool slightly.

Assemble your burgers by placing each patty on a toasted bun. Add your favorite toppings such as lettuce, tomato, onion, avocado, and condiments like vegan mayo, ketchup, or mustard.

Serve "The Zesty Zucchini" vegan burgers with a side of crispy baked potato wedges, a fresh salad, or any other accompaniments you prefer.

Spicy Sriracha

INGREDIENTS:
FOR THE BURGER PATTY:

1 can (15 ounces or 425g) black beans, drained and rinsed
1/2 cup cooked quinoa
1/4 cup bread crumbs (use gluten-free bread crumbs if needed)
2 tablespoons ground flaxseed mixed with 3 tablespoons water (flax egg)
2 tablespoons sriracha sauce (adjust to taste)
1 tablespoon soy sauce or tamari
1 tablespoon tomato paste
1 teaspoon smoked paprika
1/2 teaspoon garlic powder
1/2 teaspoon onion powder
Salt and pepper to taste

FOR THE BURGER TOPPINGS AND ASSEMBLY:

Burger buns
Lettuce leaves
Sliced tomatoes
Sliced red onion
Avocado slices
Vegan mayo or sriracha mayo (optional)

INSTRUCTIONS:

In a large mixing bowl, mash the black beans using a fork or potato masher until they are mostly mashed but still have some texture.

Add the cooked quinoa, bread crumbs, flax egg, sriracha sauce, soy sauce or tamari, tomato paste, smoked paprika, garlic powder, onion powder, salt, and pepper to the bowl. Mix well until all ingredients are evenly combined.

Shape the mixture into equal-sized patties of your desired size and thickness.

Heat a non-stick skillet or grill pan over medium heat. Lightly grease the pan with oil or cooking spray.

Place the burger patties onto the preheated pan and cook for about 4-5 minutes on each side, or until they develop a crispy exterior and are heated through.

While the patties are cooking, you can toast the burger buns if desired.

Once the patties are cooked, remove them from the heat and let them cool slightly.

Assemble your burgers by placing each patty on a toasted bun. Add lettuce leaves, sliced tomatoes, sliced red onion, avocado slices, and any other toppings you desire. You can also spread some vegan mayo or sriracha mayo on the buns for extra flavor.

Serve "The Spicy Sriracha" vegan burgers with a side of sweet potato fries, coleslaw, or any other accompaniments you prefer.

Mediterranean Marvel

INGREDIENTS:
FOR THE BURGER PATTY:

1 can (15 ounces or 425g) chickpeas, drained and rinsed
1/2 cup cooked quinoa
1/4 cup breadcrumbs (use gluten-free breadcrumbs if needed)
2 tablespoons ground flaxseed mixed with 3 tablespoons water (flax egg)
2 tablespoons chopped sun-dried tomatoes
2 tablespoons chopped Kalamata olives
1 tablespoon lemon juice
1 teaspoon dried oregano
1 teaspoon dried basil
1/2 teaspoon garlic powder
Salt and pepper to taste

FOR THE BURGER TOPPINGS AND ASSEMBLY:

Burger buns
Lettuce leaves
Sliced tomatoes
Sliced red onion
Cucumber slices
Vegan tzatziki sauce or hummus
Fresh parsley (optional, for garnish)

INSTRUCTIONS:

In a food processor, pulse the chickpeas until they are partially mashed but still have some texture.

Transfer the mashed chickpeas to a large mixing bowl. Add the cooked quinoa, breadcrumbs, flax egg, chopped sun-dried tomatoes, chopped Kalamata olives, lemon juice, dried oregano, dried basil, garlic powder, salt, and pepper. Mix well until all ingredients are evenly combined.

Shape the mixture into equal-sized patties of your desired size and thickness.

Heat a non-stick skillet or grill pan over medium heat. Lightly grease the pan with oil or cooking spray.

Place the burger patties onto the preheated pan and cook for about 4-5 minutes on each side, or until they develop a crispy exterior and are heated through.

While the patties are cooking, you can toast the burger buns if desired.

Once the patties are cooked, remove them from the heat and let them cool slightly.

Assemble your burgers by placing each patty on a toasted bun. Add lettuce leaves, sliced tomatoes, sliced red onion, cucumber slices, and any other toppings you desire. You can also spread vegan tzatziki sauce or hummus on the buns for a Mediterranean touch.

Garnish "The Mediterranean Marvel" vegan burgers with fresh parsley, if desired.

Serve with a side of Greek salad, roasted potatoes, or any other Mediterranean-inspired accompaniments you prefer.

Thai Fusion

INGREDIENTS:
FOR THE BURGER PATTY:

1 can (15 ounces or 425g) chickpeas, drained and rinsed
1/2 cup cooked brown rice
1/4 cup breadcrumbs (use gluten-free breadcrumbs if needed)
2 tablespoons ground flaxseed mixed with 3 tablespoons water (flax egg)
2 tablespoons soy sauce or tamari
2 tablespoons fresh cilantro, chopped
1 tablespoon Thai red curry paste
1 tablespoon lime juice
1 teaspoon grated ginger
1/2 teaspoon garlic powder
Salt and pepper to taste

FOR THE BURGER TOPPINGS AND ASSEMBLY:

Burger buns
Lettuce leaves
Sliced cucumber
Sliced red onion
Fresh cilantro leaves
Sriracha mayo or peanut sauce (optional)

INSTRUCTIONS:

In a food processor, pulse the chickpeas until they are partially mashed but still have some texture.

Transfer the mashed chickpeas to a large mixing bowl. Add the cooked brown rice, breadcrumbs, flax egg, soy sauce or tamari, chopped cilantro, Thai red curry paste, lime juice, grated ginger, garlic powder, salt, and pepper. Mix well until all ingredients are evenly combined.

Shape the mixture into equal-sized patties of your desired size and thickness.

Heat a non-stick skillet or grill pan over medium heat. Lightly grease the pan with oil or cooking spray.

Place the burger patties onto the preheated pan and cook for about 4-5 minutes on each side, or until they develop a crispy exterior and are heated through.

While the patties are cooking, you can toast the burger buns if desired.

Once the patties are cooked, remove them from the heat and let them cool slightly.

Assemble your burgers by placing each patty on a toasted bun. Add lettuce leaves, sliced cucumber, sliced red onion, fresh cilantro leaves, and any other toppings you desire. You can also drizzle some sriracha mayo or peanut sauce on the buns for an extra Thai-inspired kick.

Serve "The Thai Fusion" vegan burgers with a side of Thai-style slaw, sweet potato fries, or any other Thai-influenced accompaniments you prefer.

Mexican Fiesta

INGREDIENTS:
FOR THE BURGER PATTY:

1 can (15 ounces or 425g) black beans, drained and rinsed
1/2 cup cooked quinoa
1/4 cup corn kernels (fresh or frozen)
1/4 cup breadcrumbs (use gluten-free breadcrumbs if needed)
2 tablespoons ground flaxseed mixed with 3 tablespoons water (flax egg)
2 tablespoons chopped fresh cilantro
1 tablespoon lime juice
1 teaspoon ground cumin
1/2 teaspoon chili powder
1/2 teaspoon garlic powder
Salt and pepper to taste

FOR THE BURGER TOPPINGS AND ASSEMBLY:

Burger buns
Sliced avocado
Sliced tomato
Sliced red onion
Lettuce leaves
Vegan chipotle mayo or salsa (optional)

INSTRUCTIONS:

In a large mixing bowl, mash the black beans using a fork or potato masher until they are mostly mashed but still have some texture.

Add the cooked quinoa, corn kernels, breadcrumbs, flax egg, chopped cilantro, lime juice, ground cumin, chili powder, garlic powder, salt, and pepper to the bowl. Mix well until all ingredients are evenly combined.

Shape the mixture into equal-sized patties of your desired size and thickness.

Heat a non-stick skillet or grill pan over medium heat. Lightly grease the pan with oil or cooking spray.

Place the burger patties onto the preheated pan and cook for about 4-5 minutes on each side, or until they develop a crispy exterior and are heated through.

While the patties are cooking, you can toast the burger buns if desired.

Once the patties are cooked, remove them from the heat and let them cool slightly.

Assemble your burgers by placing each patty on a toasted bun. Top with sliced avocado, sliced tomato, sliced red onion, lettuce leaves, and any other toppings you desire. You can also spread vegan chipotle mayo or salsa on the buns for a Mexican flair.

Serve "The Mexican Fiesta" vegan burgers with a side of Mexican-style roasted potatoes, corn on the cob, or any other Mexican-inspired accompaniments you prefer.

Curry Creation

INGREDIENTS:
FOR THE BURGER PATTY:

1 can (15 ounces or 425g) chickpeas, drained and rinsed
1/2 cup cooked brown rice
1/4 cup breadcrumbs (use gluten-free breadcrumbs if needed)
2 tablespoons ground flaxseed mixed with 3 tablespoons water (flax egg)
2 tablespoons chopped fresh cilantro
1 tablespoon curry powder
1 teaspoon grated ginger
1/2 teaspoon turmeric powder
1/2 teaspoon garlic powder
Salt and pepper to taste

FOR THE BURGER TOPPINGS AND ASSEMBLY:

Burger buns
Sliced cucumber
Sliced red onion
Fresh cilantro leaves
Vegan curry mayo or chutney (optional)

INSTRUCTIONS:

In a food processor, pulse the chickpeas until they are partially mashed but still have some texture.

Transfer the mashed chickpeas to a large mixing bowl. Add the cooked brown rice, breadcrumbs, flax egg, chopped cilantro, curry powder, grated ginger, turmeric powder, garlic powder, salt, and pepper. Mix well until all ingredients are evenly combined.

Shape the mixture into equal-sized patties of your desired size and thickness.

Heat a non-stick skillet or grill pan over medium heat. Lightly grease the pan with oil or cooking spray.

Place the burger patties onto the preheated pan and cook for about 4-5 minutes on each side, or until they develop a crispy exterior and are heated through.

While the patties are cooking, you can toast the burger buns if desired.

Once the patties are cooked, remove them from the heat and let them cool slightly.

Assemble your burgers by placing each patty on a toasted bun. Top with sliced cucumber, sliced red onion, fresh cilantro leaves, and any other toppings you desire. You can also spread vegan curry mayo or chutney on the buns for an extra burst of curry flavor.

Serve "The Curry Creation" vegan burgers with a side of coconut curry fries, mango salsa, or any other Indian-inspired accompaniments you prefer.

Falafel Fantasy

INGREDIENTS:
FOR THE FALAFEL PATTY:

1 cup dried chickpeas
1/2 cup fresh parsley leaves
1/2 cup fresh cilantro leaves
1/2 medium red onion, roughly chopped
3 cloves garlic
2 tablespoons chickpea flour or all-purpose flour
1 teaspoon ground cumin
1 teaspoon ground coriander
1/2 teaspoon baking soda
Salt and pepper to taste
Vegetable oil for frying

FOR THE BURGER TOPPINGS AND ASSEMBLY:

Burger buns
Lettuce leaves
Sliced tomato
Sliced cucumber
Sliced red onion
Tahini sauce or vegan tzatziki sauce
Fresh parsley leaves (optional, for garnish)

INSTRUCTIONS:

Place the dried chickpeas in a bowl and cover them with water. Allow them to soak overnight. Drain and rinse the soaked chickpeas.

In a food processor, combine the soaked chickpeas, parsley leaves, cilantro leaves, red onion, garlic cloves, chickpea flour or all-purpose flour, ground cumin, ground coriander, baking soda, salt, and pepper. Pulse the mixture until well combined and slightly chunky. Avoid over-processing; you want some texture.

Transfer the mixture to a bowl, cover it, and refrigerate for 1 hour to firm up.

Heat vegetable oil in a large skillet over medium heat. Shape the chilled falafel mixture into patties of your desired size and thickness.

Carefully place the patties in the hot oil and cook until golden brown on each side, about 3-4 minutes per side. Transfer the cooked patties to a paper towel-lined plate to drain excess oil.

While the falafel patties are cooking, you can toast the burger buns if desired.

Assemble your burgers by placing a falafel patty on a toasted bun. Top it with lettuce leaves, sliced tomato, sliced cucumber, sliced red onion, and drizzle with tahini sauce or vegan tzatziki sauce. Garnish with fresh parsley leaves, if desired.

Serve "The Falafel Fantasy" vegan burgers with a side of crispy oven-baked fries, tabbouleh salad, or your favorite Middle Eastern-inspired accompaniments.

Jackfruit Joy

INGREDIENTS:
FOR THE JACKFRUIT PATTY:

2 cans (20 ounces or 560g) jackfruit in brine, drained and rinsed
1 tablespoon olive oil
1/2 medium onion, finely chopped
3 cloves garlic, minced
1/2 red bell pepper, finely chopped
1/2 cup breadcrumbs (use gluten-free breadcrumbs if needed)
2 tablespoons tomato paste
1 tablespoon soy sauce or tamari
1 tablespoon maple syrup or agave nectar
1 teaspoon smoked paprika
1/2 teaspoon ground cumin
1/2 teaspoon chili powder
Salt and pepper to taste

FOR THE BURGER TOPPINGS AND ASSEMBLY:

Burger buns
Lettuce leaves
Sliced tomato
Sliced red onion
Vegan mayo or your favorite sauce
Pickles or relish (optional)

INSTRUCTIONS:

Heat olive oil in a large skillet over medium heat. Add the chopped onion, minced garlic, and finely chopped red bell pepper. Sauté until the vegetables are soft and translucent, about 5 minutes.

While the vegetables are cooking, use your hands or forks to shred the jackfruit into smaller pieces, resembling pulled meat.
Add the shredded jackfruit to the skillet and cook for another 5 minutes, stirring occasionally.

In a small bowl, whisk together the tomato paste, soy sauce or tamari, maple syrup or agave nectar, smoked paprika, ground cumin, chili powder, salt, and pepper.

Pour the sauce mixture over the jackfruit in the skillet and stir to coat the jackfruit evenly. Cook for an additional 5 minutes, allowing the flavors to meld together. Remove from heat.

Transfer the cooked jackfruit mixture to a large mixing bowl. Add the breadcrumbs and mix well until the mixture holds together. If it's too dry, you can add a little water or vegetable broth to moisten it.

Shape the jackfruit mixture into equal-sized patties of your desired size and thickness. Heat a non-stick skillet or grill pan over medium heat. Lightly grease the pan with oil or cooking spray.

Place the jackfruit patties onto the preheated pan and cook for about 4-5 minutes on each side, or until they develop a crispy exterior and are heated through.

Assemble your burgers by placing each jackfruit patty on a toasted bun. Top with lettuce leaves, sliced tomato, sliced red onion, vegan mayo or your favorite sauce, and pickles or relish if desired.

Serve "The Jackfruit Joy" vegan burgers with a side of crispy sweet potato fries, coleslaw, or any other complementary side dish you prefer.

Portobello Perfection

INGREDIENTS:
FOR THE PORTOBELLO MUSHROOM PATTY:

4 large Portobello mushrooms, stems removed
2 tablespoons balsamic vinegar
2 tablespoons soy sauce or tamari
2 tablespoons olive oil
2 cloves garlic, minced
1 teaspoon dried thyme
Salt and pepper to taste

FOR THE BURGER TOPPINGS AND ASSEMBLY:

Burger buns
Vegan cheese slices (optional)
Sliced tomato
Sliced red onion
Fresh spinach or lettuce leaves
Vegan mayo or your favorite sauce

INSTRUCTIONS:

In a shallow bowl, whisk together balsamic vinegar, soy sauce or tamari, olive oil, minced garlic, dried thyme, salt, and pepper.

Place the Portobello mushrooms in a large ziplock bag or shallow dish. Pour the marinade over the mushrooms, ensuring they are well coated. Let them marinate for at least 30 minutes, flipping them occasionally to evenly distribute the marinade.

Heat a grill pan or skillet over medium heat. Lightly grease the pan with oil or cooking spray.

Remove the Portobello mushrooms from the marinade and place them on the hot pan, gill side down. Cook for about 4-5 minutes, then flip and cook for an additional 4-5 minutes, or until the mushrooms are tender and have grill marks.

While the mushrooms are cooking, you can toast the burger buns if desired.

If using vegan cheese slices, place a slice on each Portobello mushroom during the last minute of cooking, allowing it to melt slightly.

Assemble your burgers by placing each Portobello mushroom on a toasted bun. Top with sliced tomato, sliced red onion, fresh spinach or lettuce leaves, and vegan mayo or your favorite sauce.

Serve "The Portobello Perfection" vegan burgers with a side of sweet potato fries, salad, or any other side dish of your choice.

Hawaiian Luau

Ingredients:
For the Teriyaki Tofu Patty:

1 block (14 ounces or 400g) firm tofu
3 tablespoons soy sauce or tamari
2 tablespoons maple syrup or agave nectar
1 tablespoon rice vinegar
1 tablespoon sesame oil
2 cloves garlic, minced
1 teaspoon grated ginger
Salt and pepper to taste

For the Burger Toppings and Assembly:

Burger buns
Vegan mayonnaise or sriracha mayo
Sliced pineapple
Sliced red onion
Lettuce leaves
Fresh cilantro or basil leaves (optional, for garnish)

Instructions:

Drain the tofu and press it to remove excess moisture. You can do this by placing the tofu between two plates with a heavy object on top for about 30 minutes.

In a bowl, whisk together soy sauce or tamari, maple syrup or agave nectar, rice vinegar, sesame oil, minced garlic, grated ginger, salt, and pepper to make the teriyaki marinade.

Cut the pressed tofu into equal-sized patties of your desired thickness.

Place the tofu patties in a shallow dish or resealable bag and pour the teriyaki marinade over them. Ensure the tofu patties are well coated. Let them marinate for at least 30 minutes, flipping them halfway through to evenly distribute the marinade.

Heat a non-stick skillet or grill pan over medium heat. Lightly grease the pan with oil or cooking spray.

Remove the tofu patties from the marinade and place them on the hot pan. Cook for about 4-5 minutes on each side, or until they develop a golden brown crust.

While the tofu patties are cooking, you can toast the burger buns if desired.

Assemble your burgers by spreading vegan mayonnaise or sriracha mayo on the bottom bun. Place a teriyaki tofu patty on top, followed by sliced pineapple, sliced red onion, lettuce leaves, and fresh cilantro or basil leaves if desired. Place the top bun on the burger.

Serve "The Hawaiian Luau" vegan burgers with a side of sweet potato wedges, coleslaw, or your preferred side dish.

Pesto Passion

INGREDIENTS:
FOR THE CHICKPEA AND QUINOA PATTY:

1 can (15 ounces or 425g) chickpeas, drained and rinsed
1/2 cup cooked quinoa
1/4 cup rolled oats
1/4 cup fresh basil leaves
2 tablespoons nutritional yeast
2 tablespoons lemon juice
2 cloves garlic, minced
1 tablespoon olive oil
1 teaspoon dried oregano
Salt and pepper to taste

FOR THE PESTO SAUCE:

2 cups fresh basil leaves
1/2 cup pine nuts or walnuts
2 cloves garlic
1/4 cup nutritional yeast
1/4 cup olive oil
2 tablespoons lemon juice
Salt and pepper to taste

FOR THE BURGER TOPPINGS AND ASSEMBLY:

Burger buns
Sliced tomato
Sliced red onion
Fresh spinach or arugula leaves

INSTRUCTIONS:

In a food processor, combine chickpeas, cooked quinoa, rolled oats, fresh basil leaves, nutritional yeast, lemon juice, minced garlic, olive oil, dried oregano, salt, and pepper. Pulse the mixture until well combined and slightly chunky. Avoid over-processing; you want some texture.

Transfer the mixture to a bowl and refrigerate for 30 minutes to firm up.

While the patty mixture is chilling, prepare the pesto sauce. In a food processor, combine fresh basil leaves, pine nuts or walnuts, garlic cloves, nutritional yeast, olive oil, lemon juice, salt, and pepper. Process until smooth and creamy. Set aside.

After chilling, shape the chickpea and quinoa mixture into equal-sized patties of your desired size and thickness.

Heat a non-stick skillet or grill pan over medium heat. Lightly grease the pan with oil or cooking spray.

Place the patties on the hot pan and cook for about 4-5 minutes on each side, or until they develop a golden brown crust and are heated through.

While the patties are cooking, you can toast the burger buns if desired.

Assemble your burgers by spreading a generous amount of pesto sauce on the bottom bun. Place a chickpea and quinoa patty on top, followed by sliced tomato, sliced red onion, and fresh spinach or arugula leaves. Place the top bun on the burger.

Serve "The Pesto Passion" vegan burgers with a side of roasted vegetables, potato wedges, or a fresh green salad.

Greek Goddess

INGREDIENTS:
FOR THE CHICKPEA AND SPINACH PATTY:

1 can (15 ounces or 425g) chickpeas, drained and rinsed
2 cups fresh spinach leaves, packed
1/4 cup chopped red onion
2 cloves garlic, minced
2 tablespoons fresh parsley, chopped
2 tablespoons lemon juice
2 tablespoons olive oil
1/4 cup breadcrumbs (use gluten-free breadcrumbs if needed)
1 teaspoon dried oregano
1/2 teaspoon ground cumin
Salt and pepper to taste

FOR THE TZATZIKI SAUCE:

1 cup vegan yogurt (such as coconut or soy-based)
1/2 cucumber, grated and excess water squeezed out
1 clove garlic, minced
1 tablespoon fresh dill, chopped
1 tablespoon lemon juice
Salt and pepper to taste

FOR THE BURGER TOPPINGS AND ASSEMBLY:

Burger buns
Sliced tomato
Sliced red onion
Sliced cucumber
Fresh lettuce or spinach leaves
Kalamata olives (optional)

INSTRUCTIONS:

In a food processor, combine chickpeas, fresh spinach leaves, chopped red onion, minced garlic, fresh parsley, lemon juice, olive oil, breadcrumbs, dried oregano, ground cumin, salt, and pepper. Pulse the mixture until well combined and slightly chunky. Avoid over-processing; you want some texture.

Transfer the mixture to a bowl and refrigerate for 30 minutes to firm up.

While the patty mixture is chilling, prepare the tzatziki sauce. In a small bowl, mix together vegan yogurt, grated cucumber, minced garlic, chopped fresh dill, lemon juice, salt, and pepper. Stir well to combine. Set aside.

After chilling, shape the chickpea and spinach mixture into equal-sized patties of your desired size and thickness.

Heat a non-stick skillet or grill pan over medium heat. Lightly grease the pan with oil or cooking spray.

Place the patties on the hot pan and cook for about 4-5 minutes on each side, or until they develop a golden brown crust and are heated through. While the patties are cooking, you can toast the burger buns if desired.

Assemble your burgers by spreading a generous amount of tzatziki sauce on the bottom bun. Place a chickpea and spinach patty on top, followed by sliced tomato, sliced red onion, sliced cucumber, fresh lettuce or spinach leaves, and kalamata olives if desired. Place the top bun on the burger.

Serve "The Greek Goddess" vegan burgers with a side of roasted Greek potatoes, a Greek salad, or crispy air-fried zucchini fries.

Smoky Chipotle

INGREDIENTS:
FOR THE BLACK BEAN PATTY:

1 can (15 ounces or 425g) black beans, drained and rinsed
1/2 cup cooked quinoa
1/2 cup breadcrumbs (use gluten-free breadcrumbs if needed)
1/4 cup red onion, finely chopped
2 cloves garlic, minced
2 tablespoons tomato paste
1 tablespoon ground flaxseed mixed with 3 tablespoons water (flax egg)
1 tablespoon chipotle sauce or adobo sauce (adjust to taste)
1 teaspoon smoked paprika
1/2 teaspoon ground cumin
Salt and pepper to taste

FOR THE CHIPOTLE MAYO:

1/4 cup vegan mayo
1 tablespoon chipotle sauce or adobo sauce
1 tablespoon lime juice
Salt to taste

FOR THE BURGER TOPPINGS AND ASSEMBLY:

Burger buns
Sliced avocado
Sliced tomato
Lettuce or spinach leaves
Red onion slices
Pickles (optional)

INSTRUCTIONS:

In a large bowl, mash the black beans with a fork until they form a chunky paste.

Add cooked quinoa, breadcrumbs, finely chopped red onion, minced garlic, tomato paste, flax egg, chipotle sauce, smoked paprika, ground cumin, salt, and pepper to the bowl. Mix well until all ingredients are evenly combined.

Divide the mixture into equal-sized patties of your desired size and thickness.

Heat a non-stick skillet or grill pan over medium heat. Lightly grease the pan with oil or cooking spray.

Place the black bean patties on the hot pan and cook for about 4-5 minutes on each side, or until they develop a crispy exterior and are heated through.

While the patties are cooking, prepare the chipotle mayo by combining vegan mayo, chipotle sauce, lime juice, and salt in a small bowl. Mix well until smooth and creamy. Adjust the chipotle sauce and salt according to your taste preferences.

Toast the burger buns if desired.

Assemble your burgers by spreading a generous amount of chipotle mayo on the bottom bun. Place a black bean patty on top, followed by sliced avocado, sliced tomato, lettuce or spinach leaves, red onion slices, and pickles if desired. Place the top bun on the burger.

Serve "The Smoky Chipotle" vegan burgers with a side of crispy sweet potato fries, coleslaw, or a refreshing salad.

Teriyaki Temptation

INGREDIENTS:
FOR THE TEMPEH PATTY:

8 ounces (225g) tempeh
2 tablespoons soy sauce or tamari
2 tablespoons maple syrup or agave nectar
1 tablespoon rice vinegar
1 tablespoon sesame oil
2 cloves garlic, minced
1 teaspoon grated ginger
1/2 teaspoon sriracha or hot sauce (optional)
Salt and pepper to taste

FOR THE TERIYAKI SAUCE:

3 tablespoons soy sauce or tamari
2 tablespoons maple syrup or agave nectar
1 tablespoon rice vinegar
1 tablespoon cornstarch or arrowroot powder
1/4 cup water

FOR THE BURGER TOPPINGS AND ASSEMBLY:

Burger buns
Vegan mayonnaise
Sliced pineapple
Sliced red onion
Lettuce or spinach leaves

INSTRUCTIONS:

Cut the tempeh into slices or crumble it into small pieces.

In a bowl, whisk together soy sauce or tamari, maple syrup or agave nectar, rice vinegar, sesame oil, minced garlic, grated ginger, sriracha or hot sauce (if using), salt, and pepper to make the marinade.

Place the tempeh in a shallow dish or resealable bag and pour the marinade over it. Ensure the tempeh is well coated. Let it marinate for at least 30 minutes, flipping it halfway through to evenly distribute the marinade.

While the tempeh is marinating, prepare the teriyaki sauce. In a small saucepan, whisk together soy sauce or tamari, maple syrup or agave nectar, rice vinegar, cornstarch or arrowroot powder, and water. Heat the saucepan over medium heat and cook until the sauce thickens, stirring constantly. Remove from heat and set aside.

Heat a non-stick skillet or grill pan over medium heat. Lightly grease the pan with oil or cooking spray.

Remove the tempeh from the marinade, reserving any remaining marinade for basting. Place the tempeh on the hot pan and cook for about 3-4 minutes on each side, or until it develops a golden brown crust. Brush with the reserved marinade while cooking.

While the tempeh is cooking, you can toast the burger buns if desired.

Assemble your burgers by spreading vegan mayonnaise on the bottom bun. Place a teriyaki tempeh patty on top, followed by sliced pineapple, sliced red onion, lettuce or spinach leaves. Place the top bun on the burger.

Serve "The Teriyaki Temptation" vegan burgers with a side of stir-fried vegetables, steamed rice, or Asian-style coleslaw.

Spinach Surprise

INGREDIENTS:
FOR THE CHICKPEA AND SPINACH PATTY:

1 can (15 ounces or 425g) chickpeas, drained and rinsed
2 cups fresh spinach leaves, packed
1/4 cup rolled oats
1/4 cup chopped red onion
2 cloves garlic, minced
2 tablespoons nutritional yeast
1 tablespoon lemon juice
1 tablespoon tahini
1 teaspoon ground cumin
Salt and pepper to taste

FOR THE BURGER TOPPINGS AND ASSEMBLY:

Burger buns
Vegan mayonnaise
Sliced tomato
Sliced red onion
Fresh lettuce or spinach leaves

INSTRUCTIONS:

In a food processor, combine chickpeas, fresh spinach leaves, rolled oats, chopped red onion, minced garlic, nutritional yeast, lemon juice, tahini, ground cumin, salt, and pepper. Pulse the mixture until well combined and slightly chunky. Avoid over-processing; you want some texture.

Transfer the mixture to a bowl and refrigerate for 30 minutes to firm up.

While the patty mixture is chilling, prepare the toppings and condiments. Slice the tomatoes, red onions, and wash the lettuce or spinach leaves.

After chilling, shape the chickpea and spinach mixture into equal-sized patties of your desired size and thickness.

Heat a non-stick skillet or grill pan over medium heat. Lightly grease the pan with oil or cooking spray.

Place the patties on the hot pan and cook for about 4-5 minutes on each side, or until they develop a golden brown crust and are heated through.

While the patties are cooking, you can toast the burger buns if desired.

Assemble your burgers by spreading vegan mayonnaise on the bottom bun. Place a chickpea and spinach patty on top, followed by sliced tomato, sliced red onion, and fresh lettuce or spinach leaves. Place the top bun on the burger.

Serve "The Spinach Surprise" vegan burgers with a side of sweet potato fries, roasted vegetables, or a green salad.

Cilantro Lime

Ingredients:
For the Black Bean and Quinoa Patty:

1 can (15 ounces or 425g) black beans, drained and rinsed
1/2 cup cooked quinoa
1/4 cup finely chopped red bell pepper
1/4 cup finely chopped red onion
2 cloves garlic, minced
2 tablespoons chopped fresh cilantro
1 tablespoon lime juice
1 teaspoon ground cumin
1/2 teaspoon chili powder
Salt and pepper to taste
1/4 cup breadcrumbs (use gluten-free breadcrumbs if needed)

For the Cilantro Lime Sauce:

1/2 cup vegan mayo
2 tablespoons chopped fresh cilantro
1 tablespoon lime juice
1/2 teaspoon lime zest
Salt and pepper to taste

For the Burger Toppings and Assembly:

Burger buns
Sliced avocado
Sliced tomato
Lettuce or spinach leaves
Red onion slices

INSTRUCTIONS:

In a large bowl, mash the black beans with a fork until they form a chunky paste.

Add cooked quinoa, chopped red bell pepper, chopped red onion, minced garlic, chopped fresh cilantro, lime juice, ground cumin, chili powder, salt, and pepper to the bowl. Mix well until all ingredients are evenly combined.

Stir in the breadcrumbs to help bind the mixture. If the mixture is too wet, add more breadcrumbs as needed.

Divide the mixture into equal-sized patties of your desired size and thickness.

Heat a non-stick skillet or grill pan over medium heat. Lightly grease the pan with oil or cooking spray.

Place the black bean and quinoa patties on the hot pan and cook for about 4-5 minutes on each side, or until they develop a crispy exterior and are heated through.

While the patties are cooking, prepare the cilantro lime sauce by combining vegan mayo, chopped fresh cilantro, lime juice, lime zest, salt, and pepper in a small bowl. Mix well until smooth and creamy. Toast the burger buns if desired.

Assemble your burgers by spreading a generous amount of cilantro lime sauce on the bottom bun. Place a black bean and quinoa patty on top, followed by sliced avocado, sliced tomato, lettuce or spinach leaves, and red onion slices. Place the top bun on the burger.

Serve "The Cilantro Lime" vegan burgers with a side of corn on the cob, sweet potato wedges, or a fresh green salad.

Avocado Delight

INGREDIENTS:
FOR THE CHICKPEA PATTY:

1 can (15 ounces or 425g) chickpeas, drained and rinsed
1/2 cup breadcrumbs (use gluten-free breadcrumbs if needed)
1/4 cup finely chopped red onion
2 cloves garlic, minced
2 tablespoons chopped fresh cilantro
1 tablespoon lemon juice
1 teaspoon ground cumin
1/2 teaspoon paprika
Salt and pepper to taste

FOR THE BURGER TOPPINGS AND ASSEMBLY:

Burger buns
Ripe avocados, sliced
Sliced tomato
Lettuce or spinach leaves
Red onion slices
Vegan mayonnaise or your favorite burger sauce

INSTRUCTIONS:

In a food processor, pulse the chickpeas until they are roughly chopped. Avoid over-processing; you want some texture.

Transfer the chopped chickpeas to a mixing bowl and add breadcrumbs, finely chopped red onion, minced garlic, chopped fresh cilantro, lemon juice, ground cumin, paprika, salt, and pepper. Mix well until all ingredients are combined.

Divide the mixture into equal-sized patties of your desired size and thickness.

Heat a non-stick skillet or grill pan over medium heat. Lightly grease the pan with oil or cooking spray.

Place the chickpea patties on the hot pan and cook for about 4-5 minutes on each side, or until they develop a golden brown crust and are heated through.

While the patties are cooking, prepare the toppings. Slice the ripe avocados, tomatoes, and red onions. Wash the lettuce or spinach leaves.

Toast the burger buns if desired.

Assemble your burgers by spreading vegan mayonnaise or your favorite burger sauce on the bottom bun. Place a chickpea patty on top, followed by sliced avocado, sliced tomato, lettuce or spinach leaves, and red onion slices. Place the top bun on the burger.

Serve "The Avocado Delight" vegan burgers with a side of crispy potato wedges, coleslaw, or a fresh green salad.

Sundried Tomato Special

INGREDIENTS:
FOR THE CHICKPEA AND SUNDRIED TOMATO PATTY:

1 can (15 ounces or 425g) chickpeas, drained and rinsed
1/2 cup sundried tomatoes (packed in oil), drained and chopped
1/4 cup breadcrumbs (use gluten-free breadcrumbs if needed)
1/4 cup finely chopped red onion
2 cloves garlic, minced
2 tablespoons chopped fresh basil
1 tablespoon lemon juice
1 tablespoon tahini
1 teaspoon dried oregano
Salt and pepper to taste

FOR THE BURGER TOPPINGS AND ASSEMBLY:

Burger buns
Vegan mayonnaise or your favorite burger sauce
Sliced tomato
Fresh basil leaves
Baby spinach leaves
Red onion slices

INSTRUCTIONS:

In a food processor, pulse the chickpeas until they are roughly chopped. Avoid over-processing; you want some texture.

Transfer the chopped chickpeas to a mixing bowl and add sundried tomatoes, breadcrumbs, finely chopped red onion, minced garlic, chopped fresh basil, lemon juice, tahini, dried oregano, salt, and pepper. Mix well until all ingredients are combined.

Divide the mixture into equal-sized patties of your desired size and thickness.

Heat a non-stick skillet or grill pan over medium heat. Lightly grease the pan with oil or cooking spray.

Place the chickpea and sundried tomato patties on the hot pan and cook for about 4-5 minutes on each side, or until they develop a golden brown crust and are heated through.

While the patties are cooking, prepare the toppings. Slice the tomatoes and red onions. Wash the basil leaves and baby spinach.

Toast the burger buns if desired.

Assemble your burgers by spreading vegan mayonnaise or your favorite burger sauce on the bottom bun. Place a chickpea and sundried tomato patty on top, followed by sliced tomato, fresh basil leaves, baby spinach leaves, and red onion slices. Place the top bun on the burger.

Serve "The Sundried Tomato Special" vegan burgers with a side of crispy sweet potato fries, a Mediterranean-style salad, or roasted vegetables.

Basil Bomb

INGREDIENTS:
FOR THE CHICKPEA AND BASIL PATTY:

1 can (15 ounces or 425g) chickpeas, drained and rinsed
1/2 cup breadcrumbs (use gluten-free breadcrumbs if needed)
1/4 cup finely chopped red onion
2 cloves garlic, minced
1 cup fresh basil leaves, packed
2 tablespoons nutritional yeast
1 tablespoon lemon juice
1 tablespoon tahini
1 teaspoon dried oregano
Salt and pepper to taste

FOR THE BURGER TOPPINGS AND ASSEMBLY:

Burger buns
Vegan mayonnaise or your favorite burger sauce
Sliced tomato
Fresh basil leaves
Baby spinach leaves
Red onion slices

INSTRUCTIONS:

In a food processor, pulse the chickpeas until they are roughly chopped. Avoid over-processing; you want some texture.

Transfer the chopped chickpeas to a mixing bowl and add breadcrumbs, finely chopped red onion, minced garlic, fresh basil leaves, nutritional yeast, lemon juice, tahini, dried oregano, salt, and pepper. Mix well until all ingredients are combined.

Divide the mixture into equal-sized patties of your desired size and thickness.

Heat a non-stick skillet or grill pan over medium heat. Lightly grease the pan with oil or cooking spray.

Place the chickpea and basil patties on the hot pan and cook for about 4-5 minutes on each side, or until they develop a golden brown crust and are heated through.

While the patties are cooking, prepare the toppings. Slice the tomatoes and red onions. Wash the basil leaves and baby spinach.

Toast the burger buns if desired.

Assemble your burgers by spreading vegan mayonnaise or your favorite burger sauce on the bottom bun. Place a chickpea and basil patty on top, followed by sliced tomato, fresh basil leaves, baby spinach leaves, and red onion slices. Place the top bun on the burger.

Serve "The Basil Bomb" vegan burgers with a side of crispy potato wedges, a green salad, or grilled vegetables.

Ginger Glaze

INGREDIENTS:
FOR THE CHICKPEA AND QUINOA PATTY:

1 can (15 ounces or 425g) chickpeas, drained and rinsed
1/2 cup cooked quinoa
1/4 cup finely chopped red bell pepper
1/4 cup finely chopped red onion
2 cloves garlic, minced
1 tablespoon grated fresh ginger
1 tablespoon soy sauce or tamari (gluten-free option)
1 tablespoon maple syrup
1 teaspoon ground cumin
Salt and pepper to taste
1/4 cup breadcrumbs (use gluten-free breadcrumbs if needed)

FOR THE GINGER GLAZE:

2 tablespoons soy sauce or tamari (gluten-free option)
2 tablespoons maple syrup
1 tablespoon grated fresh ginger
1 tablespoon rice vinegar
1 clove garlic, minced
1 teaspoon cornstarch (optional, for thickening)

FOR THE BURGER TOPPINGS AND ASSEMBLY:

Burger buns
Sliced cucumber
Sliced red onion
Fresh cilantro leaves
Sriracha or your favorite hot sauce (optional)

INSTRUCTIONS:

In a food processor, pulse the chickpeas until they are roughly chopped. Avoid over-processing; you want some texture.

Transfer the chopped chickpeas to a mixing bowl and add cooked quinoa, chopped red bell pepper, chopped red onion, minced garlic, grated fresh ginger, soy sauce or tamari, maple syrup, ground cumin, salt, pepper. Mix until ingredients are combined.

Stir in the breadcrumbs to help bind the mixture. If the mixture is too wet, add more breadcrumbs as needed. Divide the mixture into equal-sized patties of your desired size and thickness.

Heat a non-stick skillet or grill pan over medium heat. Grease the pan with oil or cooking spray. Place the patties on the hot pan and cook for about 4-5 minutes on each side, until they develop a golden brown crust and are heated through.

Prepare the ginger glaze by combining soy sauce or tamari, maple syrup, grated fresh ginger, rice vinegar, and minced garlic in a small saucepan. Mix in cornstarch to thicken the glaze. Cook over medium heat, stirring constantly, until the glaze thickens slightly.

Once the patties are cooked, brush them with the ginger glaze on both sides, allowing the glaze to caramelize slightly. Toast the burger buns if desired.

Assemble your burgers by placing a ginger-glazed patty on the bottom bun. Top with sliced cucumber, sliced red onion, fresh cilantro leaves, and a drizzle of sriracha or your favorite hot sauce if desired. Place the top bun on the burger.

Serve "The Ginger Glaze" vegan burgers with a side of Asian slaw, sweet potato fries, or steamed vegetables.

Peanut Butter Patty

INGREDIENTS:
FOR THE PEANUT BUTTER PATTY:

1 can (15 ounces or 425g) black beans, drained and rinsed
1/2 cup rolled oats (use gluten-free oats if needed)
1/4 cup finely chopped red onion
2 tablespoons natural peanut butter (unsweetened and unsalted)
2 tablespoons soy sauce or tamari (gluten-free option)
1 tablespoon ground flaxseed mixed with 3 tablespoons water (flaxseed "egg")
1 teaspoon smoked paprika
1/2 teaspoon ground cumin
Salt and pepper to taste

FOR THE BURGER TOPPINGS AND ASSEMBLY:

Burger buns
Vegan mayonnaise or your favorite burger sauce
Sliced tomato
Lettuce leaves
Sliced red onion

INSTRUCTIONS:

In a large mixing bowl, mash the black beans with a fork or potato masher until mostly mashed but with some texture remaining.

Add rolled oats, finely chopped red onion, natural peanut butter, soy sauce or tamari, flaxseed "egg," smoked paprika, ground cumin, salt, and pepper to the bowl. Mix well until all ingredients are combined.

Divide the mixture into equal-sized patties of your desired size and thickness.

Heat a non-stick skillet or grill pan over medium heat. Lightly grease the pan with oil or cooking spray.

Place the peanut butter patties on the hot pan and cook for about 4-5 minutes on each side, or until they develop a golden brown crust and are heated through.

While the patties are cooking, prepare the toppings. Slice the tomatoes and red onions. Wash the lettuce leaves.

Toast the burger buns if desired.

Assemble your burgers by spreading vegan mayonnaise or your favorite burger sauce on the bottom bun. Place a peanut butter patty on top, followed by sliced tomato, lettuce leaves, and sliced red onion. Place the top bun on the burger.

Serve "The Peanut Butter Patty" vegan burgers with a side of sweet potato fries, coleslaw, or a fresh fruit salad.

Moroccan Magic

INGREDIENTS:
FOR THE CHICKPEA AND LENTIL PATTY:

1 can (15 ounces or 425g) chickpeas, drained and rinsed
1/2 cup cooked lentils
1/4 cup finely chopped red onion
2 cloves garlic, minced
2 tablespoons chopped fresh cilantro
2 tablespoons chopped fresh parsley
1 teaspoon ground cumin
1 teaspoon ground coriander
1/2 teaspoon ground cinnamon
1/4 teaspoon ground turmeric
Salt and pepper to taste
1/4 cup breadcrumbs (use gluten-free breadcrumbs if needed)

FOR THE BURGER TOPPINGS AND ASSEMBLY:

Burger buns
Vegan mayo or your favorite burger sauce
Sliced tomato
Sliced cucumber
Fresh mint leaves
Red onion slices

INSTRUCTIONS:

In a food processor, pulse the chickpeas until they are roughly chopped. Avoid over-processing; you want some texture.

Transfer the chopped chickpeas to a mixing bowl and add cooked lentils, finely chopped red onion, minced garlic, chopped fresh cilantro, chopped fresh parsley, ground cumin, ground coriander, ground cinnamon, ground turmeric, salt, and pepper. Mix well until all ingredients are combined.

Stir in the breadcrumbs to help bind the mixture. If the mixture is too wet, add more breadcrumbs as needed.

Divide the mixture into equal-sized patties of your desired size and thickness.

Heat a non-stick skillet or grill pan over medium heat. Lightly grease the pan with oil or cooking spray.

Place the chickpea and lentil patties on the hot pan and cook for about 4-5 minutes on each side, or until they develop a golden brown crust and are heated through.

While the patties are cooking, prepare the toppings. Slice the tomatoes, cucumbers, and red onions. Wash the fresh mint leaves.

Toast the burger buns if desired.

Assemble your burgers by spreading vegan mayo or your favorite burger sauce on the bottom bun. Place a chickpea and lentil patty on top, followed by sliced tomato, sliced cucumber, fresh mint leaves, and red onion slices. Place the top bun on the burger.

Serve "The Moroccan Magic" vegan burgers with a side of roasted sweet potato wedges, couscous salad, or a mixed green salad.

Cajun Craze

INGREDIENTS:
FOR THE BLACK BEAN AND QUINOA PATTY:

1 can (15 ounces or 425g) black beans, drained and rinsed
1/2 cup cooked quinoa
1/4 cup finely chopped red bell pepper
1/4 cup finely chopped red onion
2 cloves garlic, minced
2 tablespoons chopped fresh parsley
1 tablespoon Cajun seasoning
1 tablespoon lime juice
1 teaspoon smoked paprika
1/2 teaspoon dried thyme
Salt and pepper to taste
1/4 cup breadcrumbs (use gluten-free breadcrumbs if needed)

FOR THE BURGER TOPPINGS AND ASSEMBLY:

Burger buns
Vegan mayo or your favorite burger sauce
Sliced tomato
Sliced avocado
Lettuce leaves
Pickles (optional)
Cajun hot sauce (optional)

INSTRUCTIONS:

In a large mixing bowl, mash the black beans with a fork or potato masher until mostly mashed but with some texture remaining.

Add cooked quinoa, finely chopped red bell pepper, finely chopped red onion, minced garlic, chopped fresh parsley, Cajun seasoning, lime juice, smoked paprika, dried thyme, salt, and pepper to the bowl. Mix well until all ingredients are combined.

Stir in the breadcrumbs to help bind the mixture. If the mixture is too wet, add more breadcrumbs as needed.

Divide the mixture into equal-sized patties of your desired size and thickness.

Heat a non-stick skillet or grill pan over medium heat. Lightly grease the pan with oil or cooking spray.

Place the black bean and quinoa patties on the hot pan and cook for about 4-5 minutes on each side, or until they develop a golden brown crust and are heated through.

While the patties are cooking, prepare the toppings. Slice the tomatoes, avocados, and pickles. Wash the lettuce leaves.

Toast the burger buns if desired.

Assemble your burgers by spreading vegan mayo or your favorite burger sauce on the bottom bun. Place a black bean and quinoa patty on top, followed by sliced tomato, sliced avocado, lettuce leaves, and pickles if desired. Drizzle with Cajun hot sauce for an extra kick. Place the top bun on the burger.

Serve "The Cajun Craze" vegan burgers with a side of sweet potato fries, coleslaw, or corn on the cob.

Truffle Tremor

INGREDIENTS:
FOR THE MUSHROOM AND LENTIL PATTY:

1 cup cooked lentils
8 ounces (225g) cremini mushrooms, finely chopped
1 small onion, finely chopped
3 cloves garlic, minced
2 tablespoons ground flaxseed mixed with 6 tablespoons water (flaxseed "egg")
1/4 cup breadcrumbs (use gluten-free breadcrumbs if needed)
2 tablespoons nutritional yeast
2 tablespoons truffle oil
1 tablespoon soy sauce or tamari (gluten-free option)
1 teaspoon dried thyme
Salt and pepper to taste

FOR THE BURGER TOPPINGS AND ASSEMBLY:

Burger buns
Vegan mayo or your favorite burger sauce
Sliced tomato
Baby spinach leaves
Sliced red onion
Vegan cheese slices (optional)
Truffle aioli (optional)

INSTRUCTIONS:

Combine the cooked lentils, cremini mushrooms, onion, minced garlic, flaxseed "egg," breadcrumbs, nutritional yeast, truffle oil, soy sauce or tamari, dried thyme, salt, and pepper.

Mix well until all ingredients are combined.

Let the mixture sit for about 10 minutes to allow the breadcrumbs and flaxseed to bind the mixture.

Divide the mixture into equal-sized patties of your desired size and thickness.

Heat a non-stick skillet or grill pan over medium heat. Lightly grease the pan with oil or cooking spray.

Place the mushroom and lentil patties on the hot pan and cook for about 4-5 minutes on each side, or until they develop a golden brown crust and are heated through.

While the patties are cooking, prepare the toppings. Slice the tomatoes, red onions, and vegan cheese slices if using. Wash the baby spinach leaves.

Toast the burger buns if desired.

Assemble your burgers by spreading vegan mayo or your favorite burger sauce on the bottom bun. Place a mushroom and lentil patty on top, followed by sliced tomato, baby spinach leaves, sliced red onion, and vegan cheese slices if using. Drizzle with truffle aioli for an extra touch of truffle flavor. Place the top bun on the burger.

Serve "The Truffle Tremor" vegan burgers with a side of crispy sweet potato wedges, a green salad, or roasted vegetables.

Caramelized Onion

INGREDIENTS:
FOR THE LENTIL AND WALNUT PATTY:

1 cup cooked lentils
1/2 cup walnuts, finely chopped
1/4 cup breadcrumbs (use gluten-free breadcrumbs if needed)
1/4 cup finely chopped caramelized onions
2 tablespoons ground flaxseed mixed with 6 tablespoons water
2 tablespoons nutritional yeast
1 tablespoon soy sauce or tamari (gluten-free option)
1 teaspoon smoked paprika
Salt and pepper to taste

FOR CARAMELIZED ONIONS:

2 large onions, thinly sliced
2 tablespoons olive oil or vegan butter
1 tablespoon balsamic vinegar
Salt and pepper to taste

FOR THE BURGER TOPPINGS AND ASSEMBLY:

Burger buns
Vegan mayo or your favorite burger sauce
Sliced tomato
Baby spinach leaves

INSTRUCTIONS:

Start by caramelizing the onions. In a large skillet, heat the olive oil or vegan butter over medium heat. Add the thinly sliced onions.

Cook, stirring occasionally, for about 20-25 minutes until the onions are golden brown and caramelized.

Stir in the balsamic vinegar and season with salt and pepper. Cook for an additional 2-3 minutes. Set aside.

In a large mixing bowl, combine the cooked lentils, finely chopped walnuts, breadcrumbs, caramelized onions, flaxseed "egg," nutritional yeast, soy sauce or tamari, smoked paprika, salt, and pepper. Mix well until all ingredients are combined.

Let the mixture sit for about 10 minutes to allow the breadcrumbs and flaxseed to bind the mixture.

Divide the mixture into equal-sized patties of your desired size and thickness.

Heat a non-stick skillet or grill pan over medium heat. Lightly grease the pan with oil or cooking spray.

Place the lentil and walnut patties on the hot pan and cook for about 4-5 minutes on each side, or until they develop a golden brown crust and are heated through.

While the patties are cooking, prepare the toppings. Slice the tomatoes and wash the baby spinach leaves.

Toast the burger buns if desired.

Assemble your burgers by spreading vegan mayo or your favorite burger sauce on the bottom bun. Place a lentil and walnut patty on top, followed by sliced tomato and a handful of baby spinach leaves. Place the top bun on the burger.

Serve "The Caramelized Onion" vegan burgers with a side of oven-baked potato wedges, a green salad, or coleslaw.

Balsamic Bliss

INGREDIENTS:
FOR THE PORTOBELLO MUSHROOM PATTY:

4 large portobello mushroom caps
1/4 cup balsamic vinegar
2 tablespoons soy sauce or tamari (gluten-free option)
2 tablespoons olive oil
2 cloves garlic, minced
Salt and pepper to taste

FOR THE BURGER TOPPINGS AND ASSEMBLY:

Burger buns
Vegan mayo or your favorite burger sauce
Sliced tomato
Baby spinach leaves
Sliced red onion
Avocado slices

INSTRUCTIONS:

In a shallow dish, whisk together the balsamic vinegar, soy sauce or tamari, olive oil, minced garlic, salt, and pepper.

Place the portobello mushroom caps in the marinade, turning them to coat both sides. Let them marinate for at least 30 minutes, allowing the flavors to infuse.

Preheat a grill pan or outdoor grill over medium heat. Lightly grease the pan or grill grates with oil or cooking spray.

Place the marinated portobello mushroom caps on the hot grill and cook for about 4-5 minutes on each side, or until they become tender and develop grill marks. Baste with any remaining marinade while cooking.

While the mushrooms are cooking, prepare the toppings. Slice the tomatoes, red onions, and avocado.

Toast the burger buns if desired.

Assemble your burgers by spreading vegan mayo or your favorite burger sauce on the bottom bun. Place a grilled portobello mushroom cap on top, followed by sliced tomato, baby spinach leaves, sliced red onion, and avocado slices. Place the top bun on the burger.

Serve "The Balsamic Bliss" vegan burgers with a side of crispy sweet potato fries, a fresh salad, or roasted vegetables.

Salsa Sensation

Ingredients:
For the Black Bean and Corn Patty:

1 can (15 ounces or 425g) black beans, drained and rinsed
1 cup corn kernels (fresh or frozen)
1/2 cup breadcrumbs (use gluten-free breadcrumbs if needed)
1/4 cup finely chopped red onion
2 cloves garlic, minced
2 tablespoons chopped fresh cilantro
1 tablespoon ground flaxseed mixed with 3 tablespoons water (flaxseed "egg")
1 tablespoon lime juice
1 teaspoon ground cumin
1/2 teaspoon chili powder
Salt and pepper to taste

For the Burger Toppings and Assembly:

Burger buns
Vegan mayo or your favorite burger sauce
Sliced tomato
Sliced avocado
Lettuce leaves
Salsa (homemade or store-bought)
Pickled jalapenos (optional)

Instructions:

In a large mixing bowl, mash the black beans with a fork or potato masher until mostly mashed but with some texture remaining.

Add the corn kernels, breadcrumbs, finely chopped red onion, minced garlic, chopped fresh cilantro, flaxseed "egg," lime juice, ground cumin, chili powder, salt, and pepper to the bowl. Mix well until all ingredients are combined.

Let the mixture sit for about 10 minutes to allow the breadcrumbs and flaxseed to bind the mixture.

Divide the mixture into equal-sized patties of your desired size and thickness.

Heat a non-stick skillet or grill pan over medium heat. Lightly grease the pan with oil or cooking spray.

Place the black bean and corn patties on the hot pan and cook for about 4-5 minutes on each side, or until they develop a golden brown crust and are heated through.

While the patties are cooking, prepare the toppings. Slice the tomatoes and avocados. Wash the lettuce leaves.

Toast the burger buns if desired.

Assemble your burgers by spreading vegan mayo or your favorite burger sauce on the bottom bun. Place a black bean and corn patty on top, followed by sliced tomato, sliced avocado, lettuce leaves, and a generous dollop of salsa. If you like it spicy, add some pickled jalapenos on top. Place the top bun on the burger.

Serve "The Salsa Sensation" vegan burgers with a side of crispy tortilla chips, guacamole, and a refreshing cucumber salad.

Asian Fusion

INGREDIENTS:
FOR THE TEMPEH AND MUSHROOM PATTY:

8 ounces (225g) tempeh, crumbled
8 ounces (225g) cremini mushrooms, finely chopped
1 small onion, finely chopped
3 cloves garlic, minced
2 tablespoons soy sauce or tamari (gluten-free option)
1 tablespoon sesame oil
1 tablespoon rice vinegar
1 tablespoon maple syrup or agave nectar
1 teaspoon grated fresh ginger
1/2 teaspoon Chinese five-spice powder
Salt and pepper to taste

FOR THE BURGER TOPPINGS AND ASSEMBLY:

Burger buns
Vegan mayo or your favorite burger sauce
Sliced cucumber
Sliced red onion
Fresh cilantro leaves
Sriracha or chili sauce (optional)

INSTRUCTIONS:

In a large mixing bowl, combine the crumbled tempeh, finely chopped cremini mushrooms, finely chopped onion, minced garlic, soy sauce or tamari, sesame oil, rice vinegar, maple syrup or agave nectar, grated fresh ginger, Chinese five-spice powder, salt, and pepper. Mix well until all ingredients are combined.

Let the mixture sit for about 10 minutes to allow the flavors to meld.

Divide the mixture into equal-sized patties of your desired size and thickness.

Heat a non-stick skillet or grill pan over medium heat. Lightly grease the pan with oil or cooking spray.

Place the tempeh and mushroom patties on the hot pan and cook for about 4-5 minutes on each side, or until they develop a golden brown crust and are heated through.

While the patties are cooking, prepare the toppings. Slice the cucumbers and red onions. Wash the cilantro leaves.

Toast the burger buns if desired.

Assemble your burgers by spreading vegan mayo or your favorite burger sauce on the bottom bun. Place a tempeh and mushroom patty on top, followed by sliced cucumber, sliced red onion, fresh cilantro leaves, and a drizzle of sriracha or chili sauce if you like it spicy. Place the top bun on the burger.

Serve "The Asian Fusion" vegan burgers with a side of sesame coleslaw, steamed edamame, or stir-fried vegetables.

Herb Garden

INGREDIENTS:
FOR THE CHICKPEA AND HERB PATTY:

1 can (15 ounces or 425g) chickpeas, drained and rinsed
1/2 cup rolled oats
1/4 cup chopped fresh parsley
1/4 cup chopped fresh cilantro
2 tablespoons chopped fresh dill
2 tablespoons chopped fresh chives
2 cloves garlic, minced
1 tablespoon lemon juice
1 tablespoon nutritional yeast
1 tablespoon tahini
1 teaspoon ground cumin
Salt and pepper to taste

FOR THE BURGER TOPPINGS AND ASSEMBLY:

Burger buns
Vegan mayo or your favorite burger sauce
Sliced tomato
Sliced cucumber
Mixed salad greens
Red onion slices

INSTRUCTIONS:

In a food processor, combine the drained and rinsed chickpeas, rolled oats, chopped fresh parsley, chopped fresh cilantro, chopped fresh dill, chopped fresh chives, minced garlic, lemon juice, nutritional yeast, tahini, ground cumin, salt, and pepper.

Pulse until well combined, but still slightly chunky. You want some texture remaining.

Let the mixture sit for about 10 minutes to allow the oats to absorb some moisture.

Divide the mixture into equal-sized patties of your desired size and thickness.

Heat a non-stick skillet or grill pan over medium heat. Lightly grease the pan with oil or cooking spray.

Place the chickpea and herb patties on the hot pan and cook for about 4-5 minutes on each side, or until they develop a golden brown crust and are heated through.

While the patties are cooking, prepare the toppings. Slice the tomatoes, cucumbers, and red onions. Wash the mixed salad greens.

Toast the burger buns if desired.

Assemble your burgers by spreading vegan mayo or your favorite burger sauce on the bottom bun. Place a chickpea and herb patty on top, followed by sliced tomato, sliced cucumber, mixed salad greens, and red onion slices. Place the top bun on the burger.

Serve "The Herb Garden" vegan burgers with a side of herb-roasted potatoes, a fresh herb salad, or a tangy herb-infused yogurt dip.

Chipotle Kick

INGREDIENTS:
FOR THE BLACK BEAN AND QUINOA PATTY:

1 can (15 ounces or 425g) black beans, drained and rinsed
1/2 cup cooked quinoa
1/4 cup finely chopped red onion
2 cloves garlic, minced
2 tablespoons chopped fresh cilantro
1 chipotle pepper in adobo sauce, finely chopped
1 tablespoon ground flaxseed mixed with 3 tablespoons water (flaxseed "egg")
1 tablespoon lime juice
1 teaspoon ground cumin
1/2 teaspoon smoked paprika
Salt and pepper to taste

FOR THE BURGER TOPPINGS AND ASSEMBLY:

Burger buns
Vegan mayo or your favorite burger sauce
Sliced avocado
Sliced tomato
Lettuce leaves
Pickled jalapenos (optional)

INSTRUCTIONS:

In a large mixing bowl, mash the black beans with a fork or potato masher until mostly mashed but with some texture remaining.

Add the cooked quinoa, finely chopped red onion, minced garlic, chopped fresh cilantro, chipotle pepper in adobo sauce, flaxseed "egg," lime juice, ground cumin, smoked paprika, salt, and pepper to the bowl. Mix well until all ingredients are combined.

Let the mixture sit for about 10 minutes to allow the flavors to meld.

Divide the mixture into equal-sized patties of your desired size and thickness.

Heat a non-stick skillet or grill pan over medium heat. Lightly grease the pan with oil or cooking spray.

Place the black bean and quinoa patties on the hot pan and cook for about 4-5 minutes on each side, or until they develop a golden brown crust and are heated through.

While the patties are cooking, prepare the toppings. Slice the avocado and tomatoes. Wash the lettuce leaves.

Toast the burger buns if desired.

Assemble your burgers by spreading vegan mayo or your favorite burger sauce on the bottom bun. Place a black bean and quinoa patty on top, followed by sliced avocado, sliced tomato, lettuce leaves, and pickled jalapenos if you like it spicy. Place the top bun on the burger.

Serve "The Chipotle Kick" vegan burgers with a side of crispy sweet potato fries, coleslaw, or a refreshing corn and black bean salad.

Sweet Chili Surprise

INGREDIENTS:
FOR THE SWEET POTATO AND CHICKPEA PATTY:

1 cup cooked sweet potato, mashed
1 can (15 ounces or 425g) chickpeas, drained and rinsed
1/4 cup finely chopped red onion
2 cloves garlic, minced
2 tablespoons chopped fresh cilantro
1 tablespoon sweet chili sauce
1 tablespoon soy sauce or tamari (gluten-free option)
1 tablespoon ground flaxseed mixed with 3 tablespoons water (flaxseed "egg")
1 teaspoon ground cumin
1/2 teaspoon smoked paprika
Salt and pepper to taste

FOR THE BURGER TOPPINGS AND ASSEMBLY:

Burger buns
Vegan mayo or your favorite burger sauce
Sliced pineapple
Sliced red bell pepper
Fresh spinach or lettuce leaves
Sliced red onion

INSTRUCTIONS:

In a large mixing bowl, combine the mashed sweet potato, drained and rinsed chickpeas, finely chopped red onion, minced garlic, chopped fresh cilantro, sweet chili sauce, soy sauce or tamari, flaxseed "egg," ground cumin, smoked paprika, salt, and pepper. Mix well until all ingredients are combined.

Let the mixture sit for about 10 minutes to allow the flavors to meld. Divide the mixture into equal-sized patties of your desired size and thickness.

Heat a non-stick skillet or grill pan over medium heat. Lightly grease the pan with oil or cooking spray.

Place the sweet potato and chickpea patties on the hot pan and cook for about 4-5 minutes on each side, or until they develop a golden brown crust and are heated through.

While the patties are cooking, prepare the toppings. Slice the pineapple, red bell pepper, and red onion. Wash the spinach or lettuce leaves.

Toast the burger buns if desired.

Assemble your burgers by spreading vegan mayo or your favorite burger sauce on the bottom bun. Place a sweet potato and chickpea patty on top, followed by sliced pineapple, sliced red bell pepper, fresh spinach or lettuce leaves, and sliced red onion. Place the top bun on the burger.

Serve "The Sweet Chili Surprise" vegan burgers with a side of sweet potato fries, coleslaw, or a refreshing cucumber and mint salad.

Smoky Maple

INGREDIENTS:
FOR THE BLACK BEAN AND WALNUT PATTY:

1 can (15 ounces or 425g) black beans, drained and rinsed
1/2 cup walnuts, finely chopped
1/4 cup breadcrumbs (gluten-free if desired)
2 tablespoons tomato paste
1 tablespoon maple syrup
1 tablespoon soy sauce or tamari (gluten-free option)
1 teaspoon liquid smoke
1/2 teaspoon smoked paprika
1/2 teaspoon ground cumin
Salt and pepper to taste

FOR THE BURGER TOPPINGS AND ASSEMBLY:

Burger buns
Vegan mayo or your favorite burger sauce
Sliced avocado
Sliced red onion
Lettuce leaves
Tomato slices

INSTRUCTIONS:

In a large mixing bowl, mash the black beans with a fork or potato masher until mostly mashed but with some texture remaining.

Add the finely chopped walnuts, breadcrumbs, tomato paste, maple syrup, soy sauce or tamari, liquid smoke, smoked paprika, ground cumin, salt, and pepper to the bowl. Mix well until all ingredients are combined.

Let the mixture sit for about 10 minutes to allow it to firm up.

Divide the mixture into equal-sized patties of your desired size and thickness.

Heat a non-stick skillet or grill pan over medium heat. Lightly grease the pan with oil or cooking spray.

Place the black bean and walnut patties on the hot pan and cook for about 4-5 minutes on each side, or until they develop a golden brown crust and are heated through.

While the patties are cooking, prepare the toppings. Slice the avocado, red onion, and tomatoes. Wash the lettuce leaves.

Toast the burger buns if desired.

Assemble your burgers by spreading vegan mayo or your favorite burger sauce on the bottom bun. Place a black bean and walnut patty on top, followed by sliced avocado, sliced red onion, lettuce leaves, and tomato slices. Place the top bun on the burger.

Serve "The Smoky Maple" vegan burgers with a side of sweet potato wedges, coleslaw, or a tangy barbecue sauce for dipping.

Printed in Great Britain
by Amazon